Trees

Teaching Tips

Green Level 5

This book focuses on the phoneme **/ir/**.

Before Reading

- Discuss the title. Ask readers what they think the book will be about. Have them briefly explain why.
- Ask readers to look at the pictures on page 3. Sound out the words together. What other words have "ir" in them?

Read the Book

- Encourage readers to break down unfamiliar words into units of sound. Then, ask them to string the sounds together to create the words.
- Urge readers to point out when the focused phonics phoneme appears in the text.

After Reading

- Encourage children to reread the book independently or with a friend.
- Ask readers to name other words with the /ir/ phoneme. On a separate sheet of paper, have them write the words out.

© 2024 Booklife Publishing
This edition is published by arrangement with Booklife Publishing.

North American adaptations © 2024 Jump!
5357 Penn Avenue South
Minneapolis, MN 55419
www.jumplibrary.com

Decodables by Jump! are published by Jump! Library.
All rights reserved. No part of this book may be reproduced in any form without written permission from the publisher.

Library of Congress Cataloging-in-Publication Data is available at www.loc.gov or upon request from the publisher.

ISBN: 979-8-88996-843-6 (hardcover)
ISBN: 979-8-88996-844-3 (paperback)
ISBN: 979-8-88996-845-0 (ebook)

Photo Credits

Images are courtesy of Shutterstock.com. With thanks to Getty Images, Thinkstock Photo and iStockphoto. Cover – Pornsawan Baipakdee. 3 – Shutterstock. 4–5 – emper71, kemper71, ST-art. 6–7 – Urban Furniture, Fotografas Edgaras. 8–9 – Goinyk Production, andreiuc88. 10–11 – Ground Picture, DrimaFilm. 12–13 – Alik Mulikov, Jacquie Klose. 14–15 – CTatiana, John Glade. 16 – Shutterstock.

How many words can you list with **ir** in them?

Answers: bird, first, dirt, thirsty, third

Trees start out as seeds. When a seed has all that it needs, a root will press into the dirt.

A shoot will then spring up from the top. It will soon be a seedling, then a sapling.

A tree will have a slim trunk in its first year. Some trees might need support in strong wind.

Trunk

This tree is in its third year. Its trunk is thicker and can support lemons.

When a tree is big, it has a firm trunk and branches. Its roots go deep into the dirt.

Tree roots can extend out a long way.
They need wet dirt to absorb water from.

A tree's girth is how thick or thin it is. A big tree needs lots of people to get their arms around it.

You can see how long a tree has been there by checking the number of rings it has.

Ring

Some trees are dormant in winter, such as birch trees. They will bud again in summer.

Birch tree

Some trees are green all year, such as fir trees. The snow will not kill them.

Fir tree

If you see a mess of twigs high up on a branch, that might not be part of the tree.

That mess of twigs might be a nest that a bird has built to keep its eggs in!

Trace the /ir/ sound to complete each word. Say the words out loud.

shirt

chirp

birthday